This Book is for Mom

By Vontavia J. Heard

This book is a gift to Mom from:

____

Dear mom, you are the bomb!

You've wiped my tears and
soothed my fears

Through ups and downs, your
patience knows no bounds

On the darkest nights, you are
my light

You chase away the monsters
under my bed and make sure
that I am warm and fed

You pick me up when I fall and give me the courage to stand tall

With your embrace, I know
there is nothing that I can't
face

This book is for MY mother,
whose love is like no other

Thank you for everything that you do. I hope you know that I love and appreciate you.

You deserve it all, the world as your stage. But for now, here are some words on a page.

MOM
I Love you mom!

"I can imagine no heroism
greater than motherhood."
- Lance Conrad

What I Love About Mom

<u>Other Books by Vontavia J. Heard</u>

All Hair is Good Hair
Chasing Butterflies
The Alphabet Book
Everything's NOT Okay
Love, Mr. Hedgehog
Don't Talk to Raccoons
The *Let's Be Bilingual* Series